MW00905543

A pair of white-breasted sea eagles

Eagles

Jill Kalz

A⁺

Smart Apple Media

COPYRIGHT

Published by Smart Apple Media

1980 Lookout Drive, North Mankato, MN 56003

Designed by Rita Marshall

Printed in the United States of America

Photographs by Robert E. Barber, Peter Bisset, Brian Gosewisch,

The Image Finders (Bill Silliker Jr.), JLM Visuals (Breck P. Kent),

Tom Myers, John Perryman, Root Resources (Kenneth W. Fink),

Tom Stack & Associates (Mark Newman)

Library of Congress Cataloging-in-Publication Data

Kalz, Jill. Eagles / by Jill Kalz. p. cm. — (Birds)

Summary: An introduction to eagles, describing what they look like, how
they raise their young, threats they face, and more.

Includes bibliographical references.

ISBN 1-58340-129-6

1. Eagles—Juvenile literature. [1. Eagles.] I. Title.

QL696.F32 K36 2002   598.9'42–dc21   2001049639

First Edition 9 8 7 6 5 4 3 2 1

Eagles

Strong and Proud

Few birds look as proud as an eagle soaring high in the sky. Throughout history, the eagle has been a symbol of power. Many armies have marched into war with pictures of eagles on their flags. Some cultures believe that the eagle is a god or a heavenly messenger. More than 200 years ago, the United States chose an eagle as its national symbol. Strong, beautiful, free—the eagle is all of these things and more. There are more than 50 different kinds, or species, of eagles in the world. They live near oceans and mountains, on the arctic tundra, and

in tropical forests. As long as they have plenty of food and space, eagles can live just about anywhere. Two species of eagles live in the United States and Canada. The bald eagle,

The bald eagle, America's national symbol

with its white head and tail, is probably the best known. The

other is the golden eagle.

Eagle Details

Despite their size, most eagles do not weigh very

much. Eagles have an average **wingspan** of six feet (1.8 m)

but weigh an average of just 10 pounds (4.5 kg). The smallest

eagle in the world is no bigger than a pigeon. The largest is the

harpy eagle. This giant bird can measure eight feet (2.4 m)

from wingtip to wingtip! Brown and black are the most

common **plumage** colors in eagles. Some eagles also have

white or colored markings. The head and neck feathers of the

golden eagle, for example, shimmer like gold. Sharp

eyesight allows eagles to hunt from very high in the air. Once

Large, strong wings keep eagles in the air

Bald eagle plumage is white and brown

they spot their **prey**, eagles swoop down and pluck it from the ground or water without a sound. Eagles have strong legs and sharp, curved claws called talons. Talons are made of the same material as a human's fingernails. These claws help the birds catch and kill their prey. Mice, rabbits, fish, and snakes are some of eagles' favorite foods. Eagles use

An eagle's skeleton may weigh as little as a half pound (227 g) or less because all of its bones are hollow.

their hooked beaks to tear their food into pieces.

An eagle feeding on a fresh kill

Dancing on Air

Many eagles perform **courtship** flights in the spring. During these air shows, a male and female "dance" together. They swoop and dive. Sometimes the pair even locks talons and spirals down toward the ground. Eagles mate for life, which means they stay together until one of the pair dies. Once they have mated, the male and female build a nest.

Eagle nests are huge. They can measure up to eight feet (2.4 m) across and 12 feet (3.6 m) deep! Only very sturdy trees or

The average life span for an eagle in the wild is 20 to 30 years.

rocky ledges can support them. Nests are made of large sticks

and mud. Eagles return to the same nest each year and add

sticks to make it bigger. Female eagles usually lay one to

Eagle nests can weigh a ton (900 kg) or more

three white eggs. In most species, the male and female take

turns keeping them warm. After 30 to 60 days, the eggs hatch.

 Newly hatched baby eagles, called eaglets, are helpless.

They do not have any feathers, just a layer of

soft fluff called down. And they cannot feed

themselves. But with good care from their

parents, eaglets are ready to leave the nest in

about 10 weeks. Their adult feathers, however, may take years

to fully develop.

White-headed bald eagles are not bald at all; long ago, the word "bald" meant "white."

A six-week-old bald eaglet

Past and Future

Even though they are large, strong birds, eagles still face many dangers. Eggs and eaglets may be snatched by raccoons or other birds. Grown eagles may starve if a harsh winter kills their food supply. But the biggest threat to eagles is people.

People once believed that eagles could carry away young children; in fact, eagles can lift only about seven pounds (3.2 kg).

Throughout the years, humans have polluted or destroyed eagle **habitats**. Farmers and hunters have shot, poisoned, and trapped the birds. During the 1960s, a chemical

used to kill insects, called DDT, caused the shells of eagle eggs

to crumble apart. As a result, few new chicks were born. Bald

eagles almost became **extinct**. But there is good news.

An eagle preparing to fly

Today, people are working to preserve eagle habitats. Eagles are now protected by law in the United States and Canada and cannot be hunted. Many dangerous chemicals, including DDT, have been banned. Because of these efforts, eagle populations are on the rise. There is still more to do, but with everyone's help, eagles will continue to soar across the skies.

Before choosing the bald eagle, the United States considered the bison, wild turkey, and grizzly bear as national symbols.

A full-grown bald eagle

Eagle-Eyed

Eagles may be able to spot prey, such as a rabbit, from as far as two miles (3.2 km) away. This activity will let you see how your eyes compare with an eagle's.

What You Need

An empty 35mm film canister or a votive candle
A large yard or field
A tape measure
A pencil and paper

What You Do

1. Set the canister or candle on the ground on its side. This mouse-sized object is your "prey."
2. Now back away from it until you cannot see it anymore. Measure this distance and multiply it by eight.

Your answer is how far away an eagle could be and still see the "mouse." An eagle's vision is about eight times better than a human's. This is why we call people who can see very far "eagle-eyed."

Golden eagles have excellent eyesight

Index

Words to Know

courtship (KORT-ship)—the time before mating during which a male and female
    eagle get to know each other

extinct (ek-STINKT)—no longer living anywhere on Earth

habitats (HAB-i-tats)—the areas where certain animals naturally live

plumage (PLOO-mij)—a bird's feathers

prey (PRAY)—an animal hunted for food

wingspan (WING-span)—the length from the tip of one outstretched wing to the
    other

Read More

Dudley, Karen. *Bald Eagles*. Austin, Tex.: Raintree Steck-Vaughn Publishers, 1998.

Gibbons, Gail. *Soaring with the Wind: The Bald Eagle*. New York: William Morrow &
    Co., 1998.

Gieck, Charlene. *Eagles for Kids*. Minocqua, Wisc.: NorthWord Press, 1991.

Internet Sites

About.com, Inc.: Birding/Wild Birds
http://birding.about.com/hobbies/
birding

Kid Info: Birds
http://www.kidinfo.com/science/
birds.html

American Bald Eagle Information
http://www.baldeagleinfo.com

INFORMATION